For my children, grandchildren, nieces, nephews and anyone who claims me as family

Dear Reader,

I have enjoyed an epic life. Hopefully, I will enjoy experiencing much more. I was born at the right place, at the right time to an incredible family. I have passionately loved and been loved by the beautiful kind caring and faithful Claire for more than 45 years. I have transitioned from the analog age to the digital age. I have enjoyed unimaginable success. I've had a few failures. I've also had some close calls and a few tragedies. I've had good times, hard times, good health, not so good health, financial success, financial failure and met scores of interesting people. I am blessed with great friends. I have seen much of the United States, most of Texas and a traveled abroad. I have 4 fantastic and successful children and am now enjoying 3 grandchildren. I have learned a lot during my life and I'm still learning. I don't pretend to have all of life's answers but I have picked up a few things that I believe will help you.

Perhaps you are starting something new. You might be a new graduate. You might be starting a new career. Maybe you are fresh off a recent divorce or separation. You might just be seeking a happier, better, more secure and confident life. Whatever your situation my hope is that you will in these few pages you will discover a few nuggets that will help you along life's journey.
Rob Mitchell

Discover your passion and make it your career

A friend once told me that you won't find fulfillment until you find your passion. I have not yet found my passion. I wish I could. If I were starting all over again, I would find my passion and follow it. I would take risks, dream big, and figure out how to monetize my passion. Now I've got obligations that I have to financially feed. I can't afford to give up the safe and secure for my dreams. Don't settle for safe. You can afford to take more risk when you're young. Do it now when you have nothing or little to lose. When you wake up one day and realize that others are depending on you for their security... it might be too late.

Stuff is nothing, lives are everything

Too many people measure success by how much they have... money, houses, cars, jewelry – stuff.

Real success is measured by how many lives have been enriched because you have been a positive part of them.

All men (women) are NOT created equal

In spite of what the United States Declaration of Independence says, we are not all equal. If it were true, you might be able to swing a bat like Hank Aaron, my daughter could make money like John Rockefeller and your little sister could compose music like Beethoven. Being human means that each individual has different gifts, different flaws, and different motivations. Embrace your gifts, your strengths and your motivations. Celebrate the gifts and strengths of others. Avoid the temptation to compare. You can always find those who are smarter, faster, stronger, richer, happier, better looking and more successful.

Being a good listener is infinitely more valuable than being a good speaker

Blowhards and self-promoters are everywhere and they are avoided. Other people are interesting and we can always learn something from them and their experiences.

People will always feel better about you the more that you can get them to talk about themselves. That is the bonus.

Manners matter

People lacking in basic manners are easy to spot and easy to avoid – don't be one of them.

Not many people are attracted to crude language, boorish behavior, and those who are dismissive of others. Good manners are also easy to spot and easy to be attracted to. Real ladies like to be treated like ladies and real gentlemen are admired. Simple self-effacing kindness is the key to being admirable. You can separate yourself from most by treating people with respect, kindness, and admiration of their positive qualities. Jesus laid it out best with the golden rule: "In everything, do to others what you would have them do to you".

Enthusiasm can overcome many obstacles

You might not be the smartest, the fastest, the best looking or the most talented. But, if you can be enthusiastic you can rise above your limitations and make a positive impression. Choose encouragement not criticism. Coach don't criticize (especially yourself). Strive to be "Uncle Uppy" not "Debby Downer".

The more you have,
the more you have to
take care of...

Enough said.

Everyone is built to play either offense or defense – know what you are

Most of us struggle for years believing that we can play equally well both ways. Wrong! All of us are inclined to be one or the other... good at offense or good at defense

How you are affects everything. Your career, your family, your love life and your friendships will all be better when you learn to play to your inherent tendency to either be on offense or defense.

Small groups control large groups

Businesses, churches, governments, schools, clubs, and sports no matter how large are ultimately controlled by a few. You will need to decide whether you want to be part of the controlling body or if you are content just to be a participant.

Work smart, not long

There are millions of chumps out there that think that working long hours is the key to success. They have little freedom and lack a balanced life. Measure performance by outcome not by time invested. If you can make a million dollars in an hour, you are way ahead of the person who takes 10 years to make the same money.

Do not work for anyone who equates hours spent working with success. These people do not understand that the most successful outcomes are the most efficient. They ruin any enjoyment that work can provide.

Working long hours is sometimes necessary but should not be normal. Always ask yourself... is the juice worth the squeeze?

Take time to do nothing

This is nearly impossible for many of us, but it's vital. Be quiet. Listen. Watch.

Make time each day (even for just a few minutes) and don't do anything. We are not made to be busy all the time. Chill!

Exercise is awesome

Exercise relieves stress. It reduces anxiety. It improves your health. It builds your immunity. It is vital for weight management. It makes you more attractive and builds your self-esteem.

Do it... just don't overdo it.

A tiger cannot change his stripes

Contrary to popular culture, personalities do not change. Liars will always be liars. Cheaters will always cheat. Honest people will always be honest. Truthful people will tell the truth. Poseurs will be fakes. Slackers will always shirk work. Optimistic people will always look on the bright side. Pessimists will always live under a dark cloud. Detail people cannot be strategic. Strategists will never do well with details. A religious conversion may change someone's outlook but it will never change their true personality. You will be happier and more successful if you choose to be with honest, optimistic, confident, strategic people. A lot of who you are is determined by who you choose to spend time with.

When it comes to government, less is best

There is nothing that government can do better than private business and private citizens. Government is inefficient, wasteful, and mostly ineffective. The less government is involved in our daily lives, the better off we are. Dependency on government will make you a slave to the whims of others.

When things get tense go "low and slow"

When conflict pops up, when emotions are running high, when voices get loud, when insults break out it is time to be low and slow. When you decrease the volume and slow down your speech, you can regain control of uncomfortable conflict. It is nearly foolproof.

Understand Personal Motivation

Every individual in a given situation is motivated by money, by sex or by power. When you understand the underlying motivation of each person you deal with, you have what you need to handle the relationship for your optimal outcome.

It is also important to realize that all of us are hard-wired to seek pleasure and avoid pain.

Chance favors the prepared

Take some time to prepare for everything... then, everything will be easier and mistakes not so common. Tests, work meetings, travel, dates, taxes, parenthood, family events, sports, cooking, personal health, and retirement all go more smoothly with some preparation. Don't be obsessive in preparation because that leads to anxiety; just be appropriately prepared.

Religion is not a substitute for spiritual health

Mostly, church is a network and cultural outlet for people who share a belief system. It is good for meeting other people who share your values and beliefs. It can provide a support network when times are tough. It provides a venue and an audience for life's special events. It is a great place to make new friends, learn values, and support others. For all its benefits, church is not nearly as personally important or beneficial as true spirituality.

Real spirituality is a private affair between you and God. Meditation, prayer, and deep contemplative thought are the cornerstones of your spiritual health. To develop spiritually solitude and silence are essential. You won't find these things at church. However, a healthy congregational

experience can enhance your personal
spiritual life and make you a better human
being.

Prejudice is a two-way street

I have learned that I am not the person that some people of other ethnicities and faiths assume that I am. I have also learned that there is plenty of prejudice that is directed at me because of how I look, where I live, how I speak, what I wear, and who I vote for. Crazy as it sounds you will encounter people who have never met you who hate you. None of us alive today is responsible for the actions of our ancestors. Never apologize for how God made you. You had no say in how, when and where you were born. Own it.

It is not a moral imperfection to be smart, good looking, healthy, determined, happy – or not. Don't apologize for your skin color, your home, your success, your health, your family, your gifts, your intelligence or your career.

Moderation matters

Addiction takes many forms. We can be addicted to work, to sex, to alcohol and drugs, to exercise, to adrenaline seeking fun, to eating, to a hobby, to pets, to relationships. Be well-rounded. There is a fine line between focus and addiction. If any activity or habit prevents you from doing the right thing or causes you to avoid responsible behavior or destroys you, your dreams, or your relationships – You have crossed the line.

Make memories

Youth, vitality, beauty and health are fleeting. Plan, take time, and create memories with people who you treasure. Fortunes can be made and lost. Time cannot be stored or stopped. Memories are an everlasting treasure.

You can't beat a buzzard in a pukin' contest

Take the high road. It isn't always the fastest route but the scenery is fantastic.

Someone always has it better or worse than you do

No matter how good you are, someone else is better. No matter how much you hurt, someone else hurts worse. No matter how rich you are, someone else is richer. No matter how poor you are, someone has less. You are not an island.

Invest in assets that appreciate

Many make the mistake of missing opportunities to build lifetime value/equity. Instead of saving, they buy things. Instead of buying a house, they buy a new car. Instead of investing in an index fund, they invest in fashionable clothes. Instead of building a business, they take expensive vacations. Most of the things we buy lose value quickly. Anything that you can wear, drive, or consume depreciates. Cars, food, clothes, travel, entertainment, furniture, boats, and phones all lose value rather quickly. However, in the long term some things will always appreciate. US stock market index funds and real estate will build wealth over decades. Even a savings account earning a little interest will appreciate. Yes, we need stuff. We need groceries, cars, clothes, and entertainment. Just never fool yourself into believing that buying these things is 'investing'.

Trust but verify

President Reagan made this statement related to dealing with the Soviet Union and their nuclear disarmament. It is a great relationship philosophy. Unless someone has proven themselves untrustworthy, take them at their word... but there is no shame in validating their information. Expect others to treat you the same way.

Character Counts

Liars, cheats, backstabbers, poseurs, and the politically expedient can prosper. But who cares? Your reputation is an asset (or a liability) that cannot be easily replaced. If your reputation's valuable, guard it. If it isn't, replace it.

There is always someone who wants what you've got

Money, health, relationships, job, stuff... it may be a lot, it may not be much, but other people are drooling at the chance to take it from you. Watch your back!

Never do anything that is motivated by guilt or fear

Fear and guilt are very powerful motivators. Politicians, salespeople, and clergy pay their bills by playing to your fear and guilt. Actions you take based on your fear or your guilt are actions you will regret.

Maintaining is smart

If you clean it, paint it, upgrade it, replace its worn parts, change its oil, lock it, and regularly use it; it won't appreciate in value but it will not depreciate as quickly and won't need to be replaced as often.

Life is good, life is short, enjoy it

Holy books should not be worshipped

The Bible, the Koran, the Vedas, the Torah and the Talmud are important but they are only considered authoritative because select human beings tell you they are. Most of these people cannot tell you who wrote the various parts, when they were written, who decided what parts were included and what parts excluded and why. They won't honestly disclose what parts are historical, what parts are symbolic and what parts are mythical. Holy books can be selectively used to justify patently bad things like slavery, polygamy, infidelity, cheating, theft, murder, war, terrorism, misogyny and racism. Make no mistake, these holy books are treasures. They are inspirational. They are instructional. They provide useful history. However, they are not God and should not be worshipped. They are not supernatural and do not have special powers. If you have a holy book use it to understand God and how the Creator inspires, motivates, and works through people like you.

Beauty fades but tattoos and implants are forever

Make good choices.

Be suspicious of anyone who wears their net worth

Excessive displays of jewelry and fine clothes are an overcompensation for insecure and shallow people. Run from the guy with gold chains, bracelets, pinky ring and a watch that cost more than his property tax payment. Run from the woman with the excessive jewelry, perfect hair, and shoes that cost more that cost more than a house payment. They want you to believe that they are someone that they aren't.

Smile

Smiling improves your attitude. It makes you more attractive. It improves the attitudes that others have of you. Smiling eases tension and makes you more approachable. Smiling costs you nothing and has a fantastic return.

Always drink upstream from the herd

Think about it.

Share yourself

Some of history's most successful and wealthy people report that their success was directly proportional to the number of people they helped make successful. You are a precious and unique creation. Share your talents. Share your experience. Share your insights. Take pleasure in developing the talent of others. Encourage, motivate, inspire.

Look for mentors

Find people you respect, admire and trust and ask them to mentor you. Mentoring involves finding and developing your strengths. Mentoring involves teaching. Mentoring includes criticizing and correction. Mentoring works best if you are transparent. A real mentor may only happen once or twice in your life. Treasure the time.

Anger is deadly

Anger is the epitome of selfishness and ego. Anger will harm your health. Anger will destroy your relationships. Anger can torpedo your career. Repressing it is bad. Letting it out is bad. Channeling it is bad. Better to let it go. Replace it with acknowledgement and acceptance.

Places are important

Rome, Jerusalem, Normandy, and Washington DC are special. Never underestimate the power of place. Every event in life has a stage. Each act has a set. Respect and revere the importance of place in your life.

It's not the problem, it's how you react to it

Not everything goes right. People will disappoint you. Success will abandon you. Tires go flat. Markets retreat. The weather changes. How you react reflects who you really are and what you really believe.

Life is not fair – Deal with it

We all want an even playing field. We want impartial judges. We want the same pay for the same work. We want equal opportunities. We inherently want everything to be 'fair' in the world. It's best to assume that nothing in this life is fair. Be honest. Perform your best. Treat others as you wish to be treated. Don't waste time whining about fairness.

Life revolves around Relationships

"It's not what you know, it's who you know". It's more than a cliché, it's a verity of life. Your connections with family, friends, coworkers, classmates, church members, club members, teachers... anyone you know or have known will determine the trajectory of your home life, your career, your wealth, your health and your happiness. Treasure your relationships. Spend time everyday nurturing them. Call, text, email, visit and write people you care about – someday you will need them or they will need you.

Fix your oxygen mask before helping others

People are great – except when they're not. Our tendency is to trust others. Doctors, partners, friends, siblings, lawyers, co-workers and government officials are all people you will think you can count on to do right by you. And, they will some or most of the time. But they will also let you down or abandon you – often at the time you need them most. You are the only person who will always look out for your own best interests. Others will follow their own motivations for money, sex, and power at your expense. Always take care of yourself. Your money, your health, your emotional well-being, your possessions and your reputation only belong to you. Guard them dearly. Always remember to take care of yourself first. Only take the risks whose consequences you are prepared to live with. You are always the most important person in your life. Live well.

**The End
(It's just the
beginning)**